Ice Cream and Sorbet

ROMAIN PAGES PUBLISHING

Contents

Introduction 4

Savoury ice creams, sorbets and granitas 6

Ice creams and frozen yogurt 14

Sorbets 48

Frozen desserts 68

Granitas and ices 76

Index 94

Ice Cream and Sorbet

by **Cécile LE HINGRAT**
Photographs : Jean-Pierre DUVAL

ROMAIN PAGES PUBLISHING

Introduction

Iced desserts are not something new. Nero loved crushed fruit, flavoured with honey and mixed with snow. Later, in the thirteenth century, Marco Polo returned from China with an invention that consisted of pouring a mixture of snow and saltpetre over the outside of recipients filled with syrup. In the sixteenth century, sorbets were in fashion throughout Europe.

Sorbets are always made with water, sugar and fruit purée, although you can find variations based on herb teas and even wine and spirits. Sherbets include some dairy. Ice creams are based on dairy products such as cream, milk and, more recently, yogurt.

We may be used to sweet ice creams and sorbets, but they are also delicious savoury. A small ball of tomato and basil sorbet is a pleasant, refreshing summer starter.

Let yourself be guided through this book to learn various ways to enjoy ice creams and sorbets, and the art of making delicious accompaniments.

This book covers:
– ice creams made with a custard sauce that may or may not include additional cream;
– sorbets, made with raw and cooked fruit, mixed with syrup;
– ices and ice lollies (popsicles), mixed with fruit juices and syrup and put directly in the freezer (no ice cream maker involved)
– granitas which, like the above, do not require an ice cream maker, but need to be scraped.

Choosing an ice cream machine

There are three types of ice cream machines, with more or less complex refrigeration systems:
– Simple freezer-unit machines have a bowl and a motor, which you place in the freezer while it is running.
– Counter-top machines have a refrigerated bowl you freeze ahead of time so the cold then spreads as the paddles stir your mixture.
– Built-in freezer machines have their own refrigeration systems.

What you choose as an ice cream machine will depend on how often you want to use it. Machines with built-in freezing mechanisms are a lot more expensive than simple freezer-unit machines.

Different machines have different settings: follow the manufacturer's instructions. In each recipe, we indicate: "Pour the preparation into the ice cream machine and freeze according to manufacturer's instructions." The process could last several hours. When the cycle is completed, we recommend that you transfer the ice cream to the recipient of your choice (or leave it in the ice cream maker if you can) and then to freeze it for three hours.

Can you make ice cream without a machine?

Yes, you can! Making ice cream without a machine takes time, and you have to blend the ice cream manually several times: first after an hour, and then every hour and a half until you get the consistency of ice cream.

Tips

To make creamy ice cream

For a creamier consistency:
– Add a little cornflour (cornstarch) to your custard sauce, when you add the eggs.
– Use honey instead of sugar.
– Add an egg white, whipped until stiff, during the churning process.

Use whole milk over skim milk to make a creamier, more flavourful, and also richer ice cream.
Generally speaking, the more water found in the ice cream, the harder it will be and the more it will tend to crystallize. Dry your fruit well before adding.

To get ice cream to freeze well

Make sure the preparation is quite cold before churning it.

To save a custard sauce

Watch that custard sauce. It is well known that when it boils, it is ruined! But not all is lost! You can save your custard sauce by blending it in a food processor for a few minutes or put it as quickly as possible in a hermetically sealed bottle and shake it energetically. Then return it to a cold recipient, and it should become smooth again.

To avoid this kind of problem, add a little cornflour (cornstarch) to the eggs. This will keep the custard from going lumpy when it is cooked.

Important note

Ice creams and sorbets spoil in a few weeks: they lose their flavours and crystallize. We recommend you keep them in the freezer at -18°C/-65°F. Do not make too much at a time, and eat them quickly or invite a lot of friends over to eat them.

To appreciate all the flavours and textures, remove the ice cream from the freezer 10 to 15 minutes before serving. Return it to the freezer immediately after serving so it does not later crystallize.

Sorbet and ice cream are good for you

Sorbets are rich in fruits, adding vitamins, fibre, minerals and antioxidants to your diet, helping your body fight outside aggressions and regenerate itself.

Ice cream is an excellent milk product supplying a large quantity of calcium.

Let your imagination loose and invent yourself new combinations of flavours and textures!

Ingredients

- 600 g/1 lb 5 oz fresh tomatoes
- 20 g/⅔ oz/1 tbsp sugar
- 1 egg white
- ¼ bunch fresh basil
- salt, pepper

SERVES: 6
PREPARATION: 10 MIN
COOKING: 5 MIN

Aubergine bread:

- 1 kg/2 lb 3 oz aubergines (eggplants)
- 4 eggs
- 30 cl/10 fl oz/1 ¼ c heavy or double cream
- butter for the mould
- 2 onions
- 1 clove garlic
- 1 pinch ground cumin
- 2 tbsp olive oil
- salt, pepper

SERVES: 6 TO 8
PREPARATION: 10 MIN
COOKING: 45 MIN

Tomato and Basil Sorbet

1 . To peel the tomatoes, bring water to a boil (enough to cover the tomatoes entirely), and dip the tomatoes in the boiling water for 10 seconds, then run them immediately under cold water. Peel the tomatoes, cut them in half and remove the seeds. Refrigerate.

2 . Heat the sugar with 60 cl/20 fl oz/2 ⅕ cups of water in a saucepan. Remove from heat when it begins to boil and cool for an hour.

3 . During this time, beat the egg white with a pinch of salt until stiff but not dry. Set aside. Chop half of the basil.

4 . Add the syrup to the tomatoes, along with the egg white and the chopped basil. Season with pepper and mix well.

5 . Pour the preparation into an ice cream maker and freeze according to manufacturer's instructions. When ready, store in the freeze for at least 3 hours.

6 . Serve sprinkled with the remaining chopped basil leaves and a slice of aubergine bread.

Aubergine bread

1 . Peel and slice the onions. Peel and crush the garlic. Peel and dice the aubergines.

2 . Cook the aubergines in the olive oil with the sliced onions. Add the crushed garlic. Cook until tender.

3 . Blend the vegetables with a handheld food processor. Remove from heat, add the eggs, the cream, the ground cumin, salt and pepper.

4 . Pour into a butter loaf pan. Bake in a water bath at 180°C/350°F/gas mark 4 for 45 minutes.

Clementine and Tarragon Sorbet

1. Clean and chop the tarragon leaves.

2. Mix the sugar and the clementine juice, and heat in a saucepan until the sugar melts.

3. Remove from heat. Add the tarragon and the lemon juice. Cool to room temperature and refrigerate for 1 or 2 hours.

4. Pour the preparation into an ice cream maker and freeze according to manufacturer's instructions.

5. Transfer the sorbet into small recipients the shape of your choice and freeze for at least 3 hours.

6. Serve with salmon tartar.

- 25 cl/8 ½ fl oz/ 1 c clementine juice
- 2 tsp sugar
- 1 tbsp fresh tarragon
- juice of ½ lemon

SERVES: 6
PREPARATION: 10 MIN
COOKING: 10 MIN

Salmon tartar:

- 600 g/1 lb 5 oz fresh salmon
- juice of 1 lemon
- 3 tbsp olive oil
- salt
- pepper

SERVES: 6
PREPARATION: 10 MIN
START 2 HRS AHEAD
OF TIME

Salmon Tartar

1. Cut the salmon fillet into a small dice.

2. Sprinkle with olive oil. Season generously with salt and pepper.

3. Refrigerate for at least 2 hours.

4. Sprinkle with lemon juice a few minutes before serving.

Ingredients

- 2 large avocados
- ½ smooth yogurt
- a few drops Tabasco sauce
- 2 tbsp lemon juice
- salt, pepper

Accompaniment:

- 6 slices smoked salmon
- 24 large shrimp
- a few sprigs fresh coriander leaves (cilantro)

SERVES: **6**
PREPARATION: **10** MIN

Avocado Sherbet, Shrimp and Smoked Salmon

1 . Peel the avocados, cut in two and remove the pits. Cut into large cubes. Clean and then chop the coriander.

2 . Put the avocado, the lemon juice, yogurt, Tabasco sauce, salt, and pepper in a food processor. Process for a few minutes until smooth.

3 . Pour the preparation into an ice cream maker and freeze according to manufacturer's instructions. Transfer the ice cream into a recipient and freeze for at least 3 hours.

4 . Just before serving, put a scoop in each plate, surround with four shrimp and a slice of smoked salmon. Sprinkle with chopped coriander leaves.

Did you know?

Avocados have a lot of calories (140 kilocalories for 100 g/3 ½ oz). They are particularly rich in monounsaturated lipids, which are good for the cardiovascular system and blood circulation. They contain vitamins B and E, which help fight aging.

Tips and Tricks

When shopping, choose avocados that are still hard; this is a sign that they are fresh. In fact, they ripen once they have been picked, in contact with ethylene, a gas that is found in air. To ripen avocados faster, store them with bananas or apples, which naturally give off ethylene. Avoid cutting open avocados too far in advance, as they turn brown in contact with the air. Counter this by rubbing them with lemon juice. Never put them near citrus fruit, as this will cause them to brown.

- 300 g/10 ½ oz pitted black olives
- 4 anchovy fillets in oil
- 2 tbsp sun-dried tomatoes
- 1 clove garlic
- 1 tbsp capers in vinegar
- pepper

SERVES: 6 TO 8
PREPARATION: 10 MIN

Cold bell pepper soup:

- 4 red bell peppers
- 4 tomatoes
- 30 cl/10 fl oz/ 1 ¼ c whipping cream
- 2 tsp curry powder
- 50 cl/1 pt/2 c chicken stock
- salt, pepper

SERVES: 6 TO 8
PREPARATION: 20 MIN
COOKING: 35 MIN

Tapanade Granita

1 . Put the olives, anchovies, capers, dried tomatoes and 20 cl/6 ¾ fl oz/⅘ cup water in a food processor. Peel the garlic, crush and add to the mixture. Process for a few minutes until smooth. Season with pepper.

2 . Freeze the mixture for about 1 ½ hours. Scrape and stir with a fork, crushing any lumps, and return to the freezer. Repeat the operation after a half an hour.

3 . Serve in small glasses with the cold bell pepper soup.

Cold Bell Pepper Soup

1 . To peel the tomatoes, bring water to a boil (enough to cover the tomatoes entirely), and dip the tomatoes in the boiling water for 10 seconds, then run them immediately under cold water. Peel the tomatoes, cut them in half and remove the seeds. Refrigerate.

2 . Wash the bell peppers and put them in a baking dish. Grill them in the oven (under the broiler) for about 30 minutes, turning them regularly so that the skin blackens evenly. Put them in a plastic food storage bag for 15 minutes. Peel and remove the seeds.

3 . Blend the bell peppers, tomatoes, cream and chicken stop with a food processor. Add the curry powder, salt and pepper. Serve cold.

Ingredients

- 120 g/4 ½ oz/heaped ½ c sugar
- 6 egg yolks
- 10 cl/3 ⅓ fl oz/⅖ c heavy or double whole cream
- 2 vanilla pods
- 40 cl/13 ⅓ fl oz/ 1 ⅔ c milk

MAKES 50 CL/1 PT/2 C
PREPARATION: 15 MIN
COOKING: ABOUT 20 MIN

Pear and chocolate crumble:

- 8 pears
- 100 g/3 ½ oz dark chocolate
- 100 g/3 ½ oz/⅘ c flour
- 100 g/3 ½ oz/½ c sugar
- 100 g/3 ½ oz/scant ½ c butter
- 50 g/1 ¾ oz/scant ½ c pine nuts
- 50 g/1 ¾ oz/ ⅓ c ground almonds

SERVES: 6
PREPARATION: 15 MIN
COOKING: 45 MIN

Vanilla Ice Cream

1 . Split the vanilla pod in half lengthwise, scrape out the seeds with the tip of a knife.

2 . Pour the milk into a saucepan, add the split vanilla pods and seeds, and bring to a boil.

3 . Beat the egg yolks with the sugar in a large bowl until thick and pale. Pour in the milk little by little, whisking continuously.

4 . Return to a low heat and stir in a figure 8 pattern with a wooden spoon. Cooked until it coats the back of the spoon so that when you run your finger through it, a clear trace remains.

5 . Strain into a bowl, add the cream and mix well. Cool to room temperature and refrigerate for an hour or two.

6 . Pour the preparation into an ice cream maker and freeze according to manufacturer's instructions. Transfer the sorbet into the recipient of your choice and freeze in the freezer for at least 3 hours.

Pear and Chocolate Crumble

1 . Mix the butter, sugar, ground almonds and flour with the tips of your fingers to make the crumble topping. Chop the pine nuts and add to this mixture.

2 . Peel the pears and cut them all into medium-sized pieces. Put in a baking dish. Bake at 180°C/350°F/gas mark 4 for about 30 minutes.

3 . Remove from the oven, add squares of dark chocolate. Sprinkle with the topping. Bake at 210°C/400°F/gas mark 6 for about 15 minutes.

Milk Chocolate Ice Cream

1 . Cut the chocolate into pieces, add to the milk and bring to a boil in a saucepan.

2 . Beat the egg yolks with the sugar in a large bowl until thick and pale. Then add the hot milk, whisking constantly. Return to a low heat and stir in a figure 8 pattern with a wooden spoon. Cook until it coats the back of the spoon so that if you run your finger through it, a clear trace remains. Pour into a bowl and cool to room temperature, then refrigerate for an hour or two.

3 . Whip the cream until if forms stiff peaks (see page 68). Fold delicately into the milk chocolate custard sauce.

4 . Pour the preparation into an ice cream maker and freeze according to manufacturer's instructions. Transfer the ice cream into the recipient of your choice and freeze in the freezer for at least 3 hours.

- 250 g/9 oz milk chocolate
- 4 egg yolks
- 100 g/3 ½ oz/½ c sugar
- 20 cl/6 ¾ fl oz/ ⅘ c whipping cream
- 50 cl/1 pt/2 c milk

MAKES 75 CL/1 ½ PT/3 C
PREPARATION: 20 MIN
COOKING: 20 MIN

Twists

You can serve up your chocolate ice cream in any number of ways: with hot chocolate, with cocoa powder, or grilled almonds, or chopped hazelnuts, or any kind of chocolate shaving. Let your imagination loose.

Ingredients

- 250 g/9 oz dark chocolate
- 2 tbsp unsweetened cocoa powder
- 80 g/2 ⅘ oz/3/8 c sugar
- 3 egg yolks
- 15 cl/5 fl oz/⅔ c whipping cream
- 50 g/1 ¾ oz/⅔ c chopped almonds or hazelnuts
- 30 cl/10 fl oz/1 ¼ c milk

MAKES **8** ICE CREAM BARS
PREPARATION: **20** MIN
COOKING: **15** MIN

Double Chocolate Bars

1 . Melt 200 g/7 oz dark chocolate in the milk and boil the mixture.

2 . Beat the egg yolks with the sugar in a large bowl until thick and pale. Pour in the milk little by little, whisking continuously. Return to a low heat and stir in a figure 8 pattern with a wooden spoon. Cook until it coats the back of the spoon so that if you run your finger through it, a clear trace remains. Pour into a bowl and cool to room temperature, then refrigerate for an hour or two.

3 . Whip the cream until it forms stiff peaks (see page 68).

4 . Roughly chop the remaining chocolate. Add the whipped cream and the chopped chocolate to the custard sauce prepared in step 2.

5 . Pour the preparation into an ice cream maker and freeze according to manufacturer's instructions. Fill ice cream bar moulds and freeze for at least one hour.

6 . Five minutes before serving, remove the bars from the moulds and roll them in a mixture of cocoa and chopped almonds.

Did you know?

Whatever people say, eating chocolate is good for you! It contains several substances that can affect your mood, and even be antidepressant and relaxing. It is also very rich in minerals: magnesium, calcium, iron, phosphorus… and it contains antioxidants (vitamin E), which slow down the ageing process.

Ingredients

- 4 tbsp instant coffee
- 6 egg yolks
- 200 g/7 oz/1 c sugar
- 20 cl/6 ¾ fl oz/
  ⅘ c whipping cream
- 50 cl/1 pt/2 c milk

MAKES 75 cl/1 ½ pt/3 c
PREPARATION: 15 min
COOKING: 20 min

Iced coffee sundae:

- 2 scoops vanilla ice cream
  (see page 14)
- 2 scoops coffee ice cream
- 2 scoops coffee granita
  (see page 80)
- 20 cl/6 ¾ fl oz/⅘ c cold
  coffee
- 15 g/½ oz/1 tbsp
  sugar
- 6 cl/2 fl oz/
  ¼ c whipping
  cream
- 16 g/½ oz dark
  cocoa powder

SERVES: 2
PREPARATION: 10 min

Coffee Ice Cream

1 . Mix the milk with the coffee and bring to a boil.

2 . Beat the egg yolks with the sugar in a large bowl until thick and pale. Then add the hot milk, whisking constantly. Return to a low heat and stir in a figure 8 pattern with a wooden spoon. Cook until it coats the back of the spoon so that if you run your finger through it, a clear trace remains. Pour into a bowl and cool to room temperature, then refrigerate for an hour or two.

3 . Beat the whipping cream until it forms stiff peaks (see page 68). Fold delicately into the milk chocolate custard sauce.

4 . Pour the preparation into an ice cream maker, and freeze according to the manufacturer's instructions. Transfer the ice cream into the recipient of your choice and freeze in the freezer for at least 3 hours.

Iced Coffee Sundae

1 . Beat the whipping cream until it forms stiff peaks (see page 68). Add the sugar and whip a little bit more.

2 . Pour the cold coffee in the bottom of each ice cream dish. Add the coffee granita.

3 . Top with a scoop of vanilla ice cream and two of coffee ice cream. Add the whipped cream.

4 . Sprinkle with cocoa powder.

Ingredients

- 30 g/1 oz/1 heaped tbsp hazelnut butter (health food stores) or praline
- 100 g/3 ½ oz/½ c sugar
- 4 egg yolks
- 100 g/3 ⅓ fl oz/ ⅖ c whipping cream
- 1 vanilla pod
- 50 cl/1 pt/2 c milk

Caramelized hazelnuts:

- 100 g/3 ½ oz/½ c sugar
- 100 g/3 ½ oz/ ⅔ c hazelnuts

MAKES 75 CL/1 ½ PT/3 C
PREPARATION: 10 MIN
COOKING: 20 MIN

Chocolate cups:

- 300 g/10 ½ oz dark chocolate
- oil
- 45 ml/1 ½ fl oz/ 3 tbsp water

MAKES 6 C
PREPARATION: 10 MIN
COOKING: 5 MIN

Hazelnut Ice Cream

1 . Prepare the caramelized hazelnuts: Toast the hazelnuts on a baking sheet in the oven (broiler on) for five minutes. Remove and rub to remove the skin. Place in a skillet with the sugar and 30 ml/1 fl oz/2 tablespoons water. Caramelize for 5 to 10 minutes, monitoring closely so the mixture does not stiffen.

2 . Split the vanilla pod in half lengthwise, scrape out the seeds with the tip of a knife. Heat the milk in a saucepan with the vanilla pod and its seed. Bring to a boil.

3 . Beat the egg yolks with the sugar in a large bowl until thick and pale. Pour in the milk little by little, whisking continuously.

4 . Add the hazelnut butter and return to a low heat and stir in a figure 8 pattern with a wooden spoon. Cook until it coats the back of the spoon so that when you run your finger through it, a clear trace remains.

5 . Strain into a bowl, add the cream and mix well. Cool to room temperature and refrigerate for an hour or two.

6 . Pour the preparation into an ice cream maker, and freeze according to the manufacturer's instructions. Two minutes before the ice cream is finished, add the caramelized hazelnuts. Transfer the ice cream into the recipient of your choice and freeze for at least 3 hours.

Chocolate Cups

1 . Choose bowls to serve as moulds and turn them over. Wrap them with aluminium foil. Oil the paper using a pastry brush.

2 . Melt the chocolate in a water bath and set aside. Use the pastry brush to spread chocolate over the aluminium foil.

3 . Refrigerate for 15 minutes before removing from the aluminium.

Ingredients

- 200 g/7 oz white chocolate
- 100 g/3 ½ oz/½ c sugar
- 4 egg yolks
- 50 cl/1 pt/2 c milk

MAKES 75 CL/1 ½ PT/3 C
PREPARATION: 15 MIN
COOKING: 20 MIN

Strawberry and white chocolate ice cream sandwiches:
- 20 cl/6 ¾ fl oz/⅘ c white chocolate ice cream
- 150 g/5 oz small, farm-grown strawberries
- 8 square shortbread biscuits

SERVES: 4
PREPARATION: 10 MIN

White Chocolate Ice Cream

1 . Bring the milk to a boil.

2 . Beat the egg yolks with the sugar in a large bowl until thick and pale. Pour in the milk little by little, whisking continuously.

3 . Return to a low heat and stir in a figure 8 pattern with a wooden spoon. Cook until it coats the back of the spoon so that if you run your finger through it, a clear trace remains. Pour into a bowl and cool to room temperature, then refrigerate for an hour or two.

4 . Cut the white chocolate into shavings using a vegetable peeler.

5 . Pour the preparation into an ice cream maker and freeze according to the manufacturer's instructions. Five minutes before the ice cream is finished, add the chocolate.

6 . Transfer the ice cream into the recipient of your choice and freeze in the freezer for at least 3 hours.

Strawberry and White Chocolate Ice Cream Sandwiches

1 . Make 4 scoops of white chocolate ice cream and let them soften slightly.

2 . Wash the strawberries, drain well and then remove the stems.

3 . Place the white chocolate ice cream scoops on pieces of shortbread. Top the softened ice cream with strawberries and push them in. Do not hesitate to cut the strawberries in two if they are too large.

4 . Top with a second shortbread biscuit and press lightly so the ice cream spreads out. Repeat to make the four ice cream sandwiches.

5 . Freeze for at least 2 hours.

- 60 g/2 oz/⅔ c grated coconut
- 40 cl/13 ⅓ fl oz/ 1 ⅔ c coconut milk
- 35 cl/12 fl oz/1 ½ c sweetened condensed milk

MAKES 75 CL/1 ½ PT/3 C
PREPARATION: 5 MIN

Chocolate-coconut balls:

- 60 cl/1 ¼ pt/2 ½ c coconut ice cream
- 24 Mikado biscuits or toothpicks
- 50 g/1 ¾ oz pralin
- 50 g/1 ¾ oz/ ⅔ c powdered coconut

SERVES: 4
PREPARATION: 10 MIN

Coconut Ice Cream

1 . Mix together the coconut milk, the sweetened condensed milk and the grated coconut.

2 . Pour the preparation into an ice cream maker and freeze according to the manufacturer's instructions.

3 . Transfer the ice cream into the recipient of your choice and freeze for at least 3 hours.

Chocolate-coconut Balls

1 . Use a small spoon to make 24 small balls of coconut ice cream.

2 . Dip the coconut ice cream balls into the powdered coconut and/or the pralin. Stick each of them with a toothpick of a Mikado biscuit.

3 . Freeze for 1 hour before serving.

Did you know?

Choosing a coconut should not be taken lightly: the fruit should be heavy, full, and have no cracks. Its eyes (the three cavities found on the shell) should be intact and not mouldy. Once open, coconuts oxidise quickly and should be stored in cold water to avoid contact with the air. A piece of advice: grate and store in a hermetically sealed recipient so that you can use it for several months.

Ingredients

- 100 g/3 ½ oz/⅘ c icing sugar
- 1 packet vanilla sugar
- 1 egg white
- 50 cl/1 pt/2 c whole heavy or double cream
- 50 cl/1 pt/2 c milk
- salt

MAKES 1 L/2 PT/4 ¼ C
PREPARATION: 5 MIN
COOKING: 5 MIN

Mixed nut biscuits:

- 100 g/3 ½ oz/½ c sugar
- 150 g/5 ¼ oz/1 ⅕ c icing sugar
- 5 egg whites
- 100 g/3 ½ oz/⅔ c ground hazelnuts
- 80 g/2 ⅘ oz/½ c ground almonds
- 50 g//1 ¾ oz/ generous ½ c chopped walnuts
- 25 g/1 oz/1 tbsp pralin

MAKES 20 BISCUITS
PREPARATION: 15 MIN
COOKING: 15 MIN

Fior di Latte Ice Cream

1 . Beat the egg white with a small pinch of salt until stiff but not dry.

2 . In a saucepan, mix the milk, double cream, icing sugar and beaten egg white. Heat to a simmer. Cool to room temperature and refrigerate for one or two hours.

3 . Pour the preparation into an ice cream maker and freeze according to the manufacturer's instructions. Transfer the ice cream into a recipient of your choice and freeze in the freezer for at least 3 hours.

4 . Serve with mixed nut biscuits. If you want, sprinkle with chocolate sprinkles, caramel bits, chopped almonds or hazelnuts.

Mixed Nut Biscuits

1 . Beat two egg whites until they are frothy. Add the pralin, the ground hazelnuts, the ground almonds, the chopped walnuts and the icing sugar.

2 . Beat the 3 remaining egg whites with the sugar.

3 . Mix these two preparations.

4 . Line a baking sheet with greaseproof paper and make small piles of the dough.

5 . Bake at 180°C/350°F/gas mark 4 for about 15 minutes.

Did you know?

As the name suggests, fior di latte ice cream comes straight from Italy. It is a sweat, rich cream-based ice cream. In Italy, people like it very creamy. Remove from the freezer 15 minutes before serving and mix before scooping into dishes

Ingredients

- 125 g/4 ⅓ oz/⅝ c sugar
- 3 egg yolks
- 15 cl/5 fl oz/⅔ c whipping cream
- 50 cl/1 pt/2 c milk

Caramel:

- 125 g/4 ⅓ oz/⅝ c sugar
- 40 g/1 ½ oz/2 ⅔ tbsp salted butter
- 5 cl/1⅔ fl oz/3 ⅓ tbsp whipping cream

MAKES **75** CL/**1 ½** PT/**3** C
PREPARATION: **10** MIN
COOKING: **20** MIN

Spiced apples:

- 4 acidic apples
- 2 tbsp brown sugar
- 1 lump butter
- 1 piece star anise
- 1 tsp four-spice powder

SERVES: **6**
PREPARATION: **10** MIN
COOKING: **15** MIN

Salt-butter Caramel Ice Cream

1 . Prepare the caramel by pouring the sugar into a saucepan. Add the salted butter and 2 tablespoons of water. Cook until amber brown.

2 . Remove from heat and add the whipping cream little by little, whisking constantly.

3 . Bring the milk to a boil.

4 . Beat the egg yolks with the sugar in a large bowl until thick and pale. Pour the hot milk into the caramel, and then add the mixture to the egg yolks, whisking constantly. Return to a low heat and stir in a figure 8 pattern with a wooden spoon. Cook until it coats the back of the spoon so that when you run your finger through it, a clear trace remains.

5 . Strain into a bowl, add the cream and mix well. Cool to room temperature and refrigerate for an hour or two.

6 . Pour the preparation into an ice cream maker and freeze according to the manufacturer's instructions. Transfer the ice cream into the recipient of your choice and freeze for at least 3 hours.

Spiced Apples

1 . Peel the apples, remove the core and cut into medium-thick slices.

2 . Melt the butter. Add the brown sugar and then the apples. Then add the spices. Sauté for about 15 minutes.

3 . Serve warm with the caramel ice cream.

Ingredients

- 200 g/7 oz white nougat
- 100 g/3 ½ oz/½ c sugar
- 1 packet vanilla sugar
- 6 egg yolks
- 5 cl/1 ⅔ fl oz/3 ⅓ tbsp whipping cream
- 50 cl/13 ⅓ fl oz/ 1 ⅔ c milk

MAKES 50 CL/1 PT/2 C
PREPARATION: 15 MIN
COOKING: 20 MIN

Mango sauce:

- 2 mangoes
- 1 tbsp sugar
- juice of ½ lime

SERVES: 6
PREPARATION: 10 MIN

Nougat Ice Cream with Mango Sauce

1 . Bring the milk to a boil with the vanilla sugar.

2 . Beat the egg yolks with the sugar in a large bowl until thick and pale. Pour in the milk little by little, whisking continuously.

3 . Return to a low heat and stir in a figure 8 pattern with a wooden spoon. Cook until it coats the back of the spoon so that when you run your finger through it, a clear trace remains.

4 . Strain into a bowl, add the cream and mix well. Cool to room temperature and refrigerate for an hour or two.

5 . Cut the nougat into small pieces and add. Pour the preparation into an ice cream maker, and freeze according to the manufacturer's instructions. Transfer the ice cream into the recipient of your choice and freeze in the freezer for at least 3 hours.

6 . Prepare the mango sauce: peel the mangoes and remove the pit. Cut the fruit into pieces. Put the mango pieces, the sugar and the lime juice in a food processor. Process for a few minutes until smooth.

Did you know?

Mangos are rich in vitamins, antioxidants and fibre; they figure among the fresh plant foods that are recommended for a healthy diet, along with melons, carrots, and green vegetables. They help prevent premature cell ageing.

Ingredients

- 12 biscuits
- 3 egg yolks
- 20 g/⅔ oz/1 tbsp sugar
- 50 g/1 ¾ oz/⅔ c chopped almonds
- 50 cl/1 pt/2 c whipping cream
- 40 cl/13 ⅓ fl oz/ 1 ⅔ c sweetened condensed milk

MAKES 1 L/2 PT/4 C
PREPARATION: 15 MIN
COOKING: 10 MIN

Cornets (cones):

- 2 eggs
- 100 g/3 ½ oz/ scant ½ c butter
- 150 g/5 ¼ oz/¾ c sugar
- 1 pinch powdered vanilla
- 110 g/3 ⅘ oz/ ⅞ c flour
- 15 cl/5 fl oz/⅔ c milk

MAKES 12 CORNETS
PREPARATION: 10 MIN
COOKING: 15 TO 20 MIN

Biscuit and Pralin Ice Cream

1 . Toast the almonds in a skillet with the sugar. Remove from heat and cool to room temperature.

2 . Break the biscuits into pieces. Beat the whipping cream until it forms stiff peaks (see page 68). Refrigerate.

3 . Beat the egg yolks in a large bowl. Add the sweetened condensed milk, the caramelised almonds and the crushed biscuits. Add the whipped cream.

4 . Pour the preparation into an ice cream maker and freeze according to the manufacturer's instructions. Transfer the ice cream into the recipient of your choice and freeze in the freezer for at least 3 hours.

Cornets

1 . Melt the butter in a small saucepan. Mix together the sugar, eggs, vanilla and milk until well mixed and smooth.

2 . Continue mixing and add the melted butter. Pour in the flour.

3 . Line a baking sheet with greaseproof paper and spread small quantities into circles. Bake at 200°C/400°F/gas mark 6 for 15 to 20 minutes.

4 . Shape cornets out of cardboard. When the batter is cooked, remove from the over and roll into the shape of a cornet using the cardboard cornets as a mould.

Tips and Tricks

Think about pouring a little melted chocolate at the bottom of the cornet to seal them.

Ingredients

- 200 g/7 oz spice cake
- 100 g/3 ½ oz/½ c brown sugar
- 2 tbsp honey
- 6 egg yolks
- 50 g/1 ¾ oz/⅔ c flaked almond
- 2 pieces star anise
- 60 cl/1 ¼ pt/ 2 ½ c milk

MAKES 75 CL/1 PT/2 C
PREPARATION: 15 MIN
COOKING: ABOUT 20 MIN

Spiced poached pears:

- 4 pears (williams or conference)
- 100 g/3 ½ oz/½ c sugar
- 2 cloves
- 2 pieces star anise
- 1 cinnamon stick

SERVES: 4
PREPARATION: 15 MIN
COOKING:
ABOUT 40 MIN

Spice Cake and Almond Ice Cream

1 . Toast the flaked almonds in a non-stick pan with half of the brown sugar.

2 . Heat the milk in a saucepan with the star anise. Bring to a boil. Remove from heat, add the honey and the spice cake cut into pieces. Allow the latter to soak a few minutes.

3 . Beat the egg yolks with the remaining brown sugar in a large bowl until thick and pale. Pour in the milk and spice cake mixture little by little, whisking continuously. Return to a low heat and stir in a figure 8 pattern with a wooden spoon. Cook until it coats the back of the spoon so that if you run your finger through it, a clear trace remains. Pour into a bowl and cool to room temperature, then refrigerate for an hour or two. Remove the star anise.

4 . Freeze in an ice cream maker according to manufacturer's instructions. Five minutes before it is ready, add the toasted almonds.

5 . Serve with spiced poached pears.

Spiced Poached Pears

1 . Prepare a syrup by mixing 60 cl/1 ¼ pints/2 ½ cups of water with the sugar, cloves, cinnamon and star anise. Bring to a boil, reduce the heat and simmer for 5 minutes.

2 . Remove from heat, cover and steep.

3 . Peel the pears without removing the stem. Place them whole, stem-side up in the syrup and poach over a low heat for about 30 minutes, until they are tender.

Ingredients

- 100 g/3 ½ oz/½ c sugar
- 4 egg yolks
- 150 g/5 fl oz/
  ⅔ c whipping cream
- 1 tsp grated orange zest
- 1 tbsp candied orange
  peel
- ½ tsp ground nutmeg
- 3 cl/1 fl oz/2 tbsp orange
  flower water
- 50 cl/1 pt/2 c milk

MAKES 75 CL/1 ½ PT/3 C
PREPARATION: 15 MIN
COOKING: ABOUT 15 MIN

Baklava:

- 15 sheets filo dough
- 50 g/1 ¾ oz/¼ c sugar
- 100 g/3 ½ oz/
  generous ¼ c honey
- 100 g/3 ½ oz/
  scant ½ c butter
- 275 g/10 oz/
  1 ¾ c almonds
- 1 tbsp ground
  cinnamon
- 3 tbsp orange
  flower water

MAKES 30 BAKLAVA
PREPARATION: 15 MIN
COOKING: 20 MIN

Orange Flower Water Ice Cream

1 . Bring the milk and cream to a boil. Remove from heat and add the orange flower water and the nutmeg.

2 . Beat the egg yolks with the sugar in a large bowl until thick and pale. Pour in the flavoured milk little by little, whisking continuously.

3 . Return to a low heat and stir in a figure 8 pattern with a wooden spoon. Cook until it coats the back of the spoon so that if you run your finger through it, a clear trace remains. Add the orange zest and candied orange peel and pour into a bowl. Cool to room temperature, then refrigerate for an hour or two.

4 . Pour the preparation into an ice cream maker and freeze according to the manufacturer's instructions. Transfer the sorbet into the recipient of your choice and freeze for at least 3 hours.

Baklava

1 . Preheat the oven to 180°C/350°F/gas mark 4. Grind the almonds roughly and mix them in a bowl with the sugar, 2 tablespoons of orange flower water and 50 g/1 ¾ oz/¼ cup melted butter to make the stuffing.

2 . Melt the remaining 50 g/1 ¾ oz/¼ cup butter. Cut the filo dough sheets to fit into the baking dish. Pile five of them up, buttering each one using a pastry brush. Spread out half of the stuffing, and top with five more buttered sheets. Add the remaining stuffing and top with the remaining five sheets of filo dough.

3 . Sprinkle with cinnamon. Use a very sharp knife and cut squares any size you choose. Bake for about 20 minutes.

4 . Heat the honey and the remaining orange flower water in a small saucepan. Pour over the baklava.

5 . Cool and then dry for a day before serving.

- 6 g/¼ oz/heaped tsp matcha green tea
- 100 g/3 ½ oz/½ c sugar
- 3 egg yolks
- 150 g/5 fl oz/⅔ c whipping cream
- 25 cl/8 ½ fl oz/1 c milk

MAKES 50 CL/1 PT/2 C
PREPARATION: 15 MIN
COOKING: 20 MIN

Pineapple and mango carpaccio:

- 1 small sugarloaf pineapple
- 2 mangoes
- 3 tbsp brown sugar

SERVES: 4
PREPARATION: 15 MIN

Matcha Green Tea Ice Cream

1 . Bring the milk to a boil with the whipping cream. Add the matcha green tea and whisk well.

2 . Beat the egg yolks with the sugar in a large bowl until thick and pale. Pour in the milk little by little, whisking continuously. Return to a low heat and stir in a figure 8 pattern with a wooden spoon. Cook until it coats the back of the spoon so that if you run your finger through it, a clear trace remains. Pour into a bowl and cool to room temperature, then refrigerate for an hour or two.

3 . Pour the preparation into an ice cream maker and freeze according to the manufacturer's instructions. Transfer the sorbet into the recipient of your choice and freeze for at least 3 hours.

4 . Serve with pineapple and mango carpaccio.

Pineapple and Mango Carpaccio

1 . Peel the fruit. Remove the core from the pineapple and the pits from the mangoes. Cut the fruit into thin slices using a very sharp knife.

2 . Sprinkle with brown sugar.

Did you know?

Matcha is a Japanese green tea used for the tea ceremony. It is ground into a very fine powder. Unlike other teas, it is not steeped, but is beaten into the hot water. Preheat the bowl with boiling water. Heat the whisk by turning it in the bowl a few times and then throw out that water. Add 2 grams of matcha to the bowl. Pour in 60 ml/2 fl oz/¼ cup of water your have boiled and cooled slightly (80°C/176°F). Whisk until frothy.

Ingredients

- 6 vanilla yogurts
- 8 tbsp honey
- 100 g/3 ½ oz black-currants
- 30 g/1 oz/1 ½ tbsp sugar

SERVES: 8
PREPARATION: 10 MIN

Frozen Honey and Blackcurrant Yogurt

1 . Empty the yogurt into the ice cream maker and freeze according to manufacturer's instructions.

2 . Process the blackcurrant with the sugar in a food process until smooth.

3 . Fill 8 individual recipients with the frozen yogurt. Pour a tablespoon of honey into each.

4 . Add a layer of blackcurrant sauce and freeze for at least 3 hours.

Lemon and Curcuma Frozen Yogurt

- 6 lemon yogurts
- 10 cl/3 ⅓ fl oz/⅖ c double cream
- 10 cl/3 ⅓ fl oz/⅖ c lemon syrup
- 1 tsp curcuma
- 4 tbsp candied lemon peel
- 3 oranges

SERVES: 6
PREPARATION: 15 MIN

1 . Pour the yogurts, cream and lemon syrup into a bowl.

2 . Add the candied lemon peel and the curcuma.

3 . Pour the preparation into an ice cream maker, and freeze according to the manufacturer's instructions.

4 . Transfer the ice cream into a recipient of your choice and freeze for at least 3 hours.

5 . Serve the frozen yogurt with orange slices.

- 12 petits suisses, or other rich fromage frais or creamy fresh cheese
- 100 g/3 ½ oz/½ c sugar
- 125 g/4 ⅓ oz raspberries
- 4 tbsp raspberry syrup

SERVES: 12
PREPARATION: 10 MIN

Caramel heart biscuits:

- 1 package butter puff pastry
- 100 g/3 ½ oz/½ c sugar

MAKES 12 BISCUITS
PREPARATION: 15 MIN
COOKING: 20 MIN

Frozen Petits Suisses with Raspberries

1 . Remove the petits suisses from their containers and put in the food processor.

2 . Set aside 12 raspberries and add the rest to the food processor with the syrup and the sugar. Process.

3 . Clean the petits suisses containers. Place a raspberry at the bottom of each one. Add the mixture.

4 . Stick a small spoon or short stick into each one. Freeze for 3 hours.

5 . Serve for snack with caramel heart biscuits.

Caramel Heart Biscuits

1 . Preheat the oven to 180°C/350°F/gas mark 4.

2 . Roll out the puff pastry and sprinkle with sugar. Roll up lengthwise until you reach half the width. Do the same on the other side.

3 . Freeze for 5 minutes.

4 . Cut slices 1 cm/⅓ inch thick. Set out baking sheet lined with greaseproof paper.

5 . Bake for about 20 minutes.

Ingredients

- 1 kg/2 lbs 3 oz strawberries
- 250 g/9 oz/1 c sugar
- juice of 1 lemon

MAKES 1 L/2 PT/4 C
PREPARATION: 10 MIN
COOKING: 5 MIN

Frozen strawberry charlottes:

- 50 cl/1 pt/2 c strawberry sorbet
- 1 packet strawberries
- 20 sponge (lady) fingers
- 50 g/1 ¾ oz meringue crumbs
- 3 tbsp strawberry liqueur or syrup

SERVES: 6
PREPARATION: 20 MIN

Strawberry Sorbet

1 . Prepare a syrup. Mix 30 cl/10 fl oz/1 ¼ cups of water with the sugar in a large saucepan.

2 . Bring to a boil, reduce the heat and simmer for 5 minutes. Cool to room temperature.

3 . Wash the strawberries, remove the stems and cut in half.

4 . Blend the fruit with the lemon juice and the syrup.

5 . Pour the preparation into an ice cream maker and freeze according to the manufacturer's instructions. Transfer the ice cream into a recipient of your choice and freeze for at least 1 hour.

Frozen Strawberry Charlottes

1 . Line small individual moulds with cling wrap, leaving some hanging over the edges. Remove the sorbet from the freezer so that it softens slightly.

2 . Mix the strawberry liqueur with a little water and dip the sponge fingers in this mixture.

3 . Use them to line the moulds. Cover with a good layer of sorbet. Top with meringue crumbs and then sorbet. Finish off with a layer of soaked biscuits. Pack well. Close up the cling wrap. Freeze for 1 to 2 hours.

4 . Remove from the mould delicately just before serving. Serve with strawberries and whipped cream (optional, see page 68).

Lemon Sorbet

- 30 cl/10 fl oz/ 1 ¼ c lemon juice
- zest of 1 lemon
- 300 g/10 ½ oz/1 ½ c sugar
- 30 cl/10 fl oz/1 ¼ c water
- ½ vanilla pod

MAKES 50 CL/1 PT/2 C
PREPARATION: 20 MIN
COOKING: 5 MIN

1 . Prepare a syrup. Split the vanilla pod and scrape out the seeds. In a large saucepan, mix the water with the sugar, zest the vanilla pod with its seeds. Bring to a boil. Reduce the heat and simmer for 5 minutes.

2 . Remove from heat and strain through a fine sieve. Add the lemon juice.

3 . Cool to room temperature, then refrigerate 1 hour.

4 . Pour the preparation into an ice cream maker and freeze according to the manufacturer's instructions.

5 . Transfer the sorbet into the recipient of your choice and freeze for at least 3 hours.

Twists

Try using this sorbet to garnish hollowed out lemons. Cut a top off of each lemon and remove the fruit from inside, keeping the rind intact. Fill with sorbet. Cover with the top. Keep in the freezer.

Pineapple Sorbet

- 1 ripe pineapple
- juice of 1 lime
- 300 g/10 ½ oz/1 ½ c sugar
- 30 cl/10 fl oz/1 ¼ c water

MAKES 75 CL/1 ½ PT/3 C
PREPARATION: 20 MIN
COOKING: 5 MIN

1 . Prepare a syrup. Mix the water and sugar in a large saucepan and bring to a boil. Reduce the heat and simmer for 5 minutes. Cool to room temperature, then refrigerate 1 hour.

2 . Cut the pineapple into six sections, remove the hard central core and the eyes. Then cut it into medium-sized pieces. Process in a food processor and pour into the syrup. Add the lime juice and mix well.

3 . Pour the preparation into an ice cream maker and freeze according to the manufacturer's instructions.

4 . Transfer the ice cream into a recipient of your choice and freeze for at least 3 hours.

5 . Serve this sorbet in a dish filled with kiwi, passion fruit, mangoes, bananas, all cut into small pieces and soaked in a little rum and sugar.

Ingredients

- 6 peaches
- 200 g/7 oz/1 c sugar
- juice of 1 lemon
- 30 cl/10 fl oz/1 ¼ c water

MAKES 75 CL/1 ½ PT/3 C
PREPARATION: 20 MIN
COOKING: 5 MIN

Almond tuiles:

- 100 g/3 ½ oz/½ c sugar
- 60 g/2 oz/generous ¼ c softened butter
- 40 g/1 ½ oz/⅓ c flour
- 40 g/1 ½ oz/½ c flaked almonds
- 2 egg whites

MAKES 10 TUILES
PREPARATION: 10 MIN
COOKING: 10 TO 15 MIN

Peach Sorbet

1 . Prepare a syrup. Mix the water and sugar in a large saucepan and bring to a boil. Reduce the heat and simmer for 5 minutes. Cool to room temperature, then refrigerate 1 hour.

2 . Peel the peaches, pit them, mash them or process in a food processor if you do not want chunks in the sorbet. Add the sugar syrup and the lemon juice.

3 . Pour the preparation into an ice cream maker and freeze according to the manufacturer's instructions. Transfer the ice cream into a recipient of your choice and freeze for at least 3 hours.

4 . Serve on a bed of red currant jam or jelly, with a few toasted almonds and an almond tuile.

Almond Tuiles

1 . Preheat the oven to 180°C/350°F/gas mark 4.

2 . Beat the egg whites slightly, until frothy. Add the softened butter, the sugar, the almonds and the flour.

3 . Line a baking sheet with greaseproof paper and top with small piles of the batter. Space them wide enough apart so they do not run together when cooking.

4 . Bake for 10 to 15 minutes.

5 . Remove from the oven and while they are still warm, drape them over a rolling pin, a glass bottle… Allow to cool.

6 . Store the tuiles in a metal box.

* 6 Granny Smith apples
* 1 lemon
* 200 g/7 oz/1 c sugar
* 50 cl/1 pt/2 c water
* 1 vanilla pod

MAKES 75 CL/1 ½ PT/3 C
PREPARATION: 20 MIN
COOKING: 5 MIN

Calvados sundae:

* 8 scoops Granny Smith sorbet
* 2 Granny Smith apples
* 1 small piece butter
* 4 tbsp calvados

SERVES: 4
PREPARATION: 10 MIN
COOKING: 10 MIN

Granny Smith Sorbet

1 . Prepare a syrup. Split the vanilla pod and scrape out the seeds. In a large saucepan, mix the water with the sugar, and the vanilla pod with its seeds. Bring to a boil. Reduce the heat and simmer for 5 minutes. Cool to room temperature, then refrigerate 1 hour.

2 . Wash the apples, remove the core and cut into small pieces, with the skin still on. Rub with lemon juice. Process half the apples in the food processor.

3 . Add the other half of the apples and then the syrup.

4 . Pour the preparation into an ice cream maker and freeze according to the manufacturer's instructions. Transfer the ice cream into a recipient of your choice and freeze for at least 3 hours.

5 . Serve doused in calvados as a trou normand between courses to refresh the palate, or as dessert.

Calvados Sundae

1 . Peel the apples, remove the seeds and cut into medium-thick slices.

2 . Cook them in a skillet with a small piece of butter, until they are soft.

3 . Remove from heat and cool to room temperature.

4 . Place the apples in the bottom of serving dishes. Add 2 scoops of apple sorbet.

5 . Sprinkle with calvados.

Ingredients

- 500 g/1 lb 2 oz fresh figs
- juice of 1 lemon
- 100 g/3 ½ oz/½ c sugar
- 25 cl/8 ½ fl oz/1 c orange juice

MAKES 75 CL/1 ½ PT/3 C
PREPARATION: 15 MIN
COOKING: 5 MIN

Maple syrup cups:

- 125 g/4 ⅓ oz/⅔ c brown sugar
- 125 g/4 ⅓ oz/½ c butter
- 125 g/4 fl oz/½ c maple syrup
- 125 g/4 ⅓ oz/1 c flour
- 1 tsp ground ginger

MAKES 12 C
PREPARATION: 10 MIN
COOKING: 9 TO 10 MIN

Fig Sorbet

1 . Wash the figs and cut them into small pieces. Cook them with the sugar and the lemon and orange juices for 5 minutes.

2 . Blend in a food processor and cool to room temperature, then refrigerate 1 hour.

3 . Pour the preparation into an ice cream maker, and freeze according to the manufacturer's instructions. Transfer the ice cream into a recipient of your choice and freeze for at least 3 hours.

4 . You can serve this sorbet with fresh figs, presented in a maple syrup cup.

Maple Syrup Cups

1 . Melt the butter with the sugar and the maple syrup in a small saucepan. Add the flour and the ginger and mix well.

2 . Line a baking sheet with greaseproof paper and make small piles of the dough. Bake at 180°C/350°F/gas mark 4 for 9 to 10 minutes.

3 . Place the hot tuiles immediately on overturned bowls to give them their shape.

4 . After a few minutes, when the biscuits are cool, remove them and set aside. These will keep in a hermetically sealed box for one to two weeks.

Ingredients

- 75 cl/1 ½ pt/ generous 3 c orange juice
- juice of 1 lemon
- 250 g/9 oz/1 ¼ c sugar

MAKES 75 CL/1 ½ PT/3 C
PREPARATION: 10 MIN

Runny chocolate cake:

- 200 g/7 oz dark chocolate
- 150 g/5 ¼ oz/⅔ c butter
- 120 g/4 ¼ oz/⅝ c sugar
- 100 g/3 ½ oz/⅞ c flour
- 4 eggs

SERVES: 12
PREPARATION: 10 MIN
COOKING: 10 MIN

Orange Sorbet

1 . Mix the orange juice, lemon juice and sugar in a large bowl. Mix well to dissolve the latter.

2 . Pour the preparation into an ice cream maker and freeze according to the manufacturer's instructions. Transfer the ice cream into a recipient of your choice and freeze for at least 3 hours.

3 . Serve in the glasses in which you have prepared the runny chocolate cake. Optionally, top with melted chocolate.

Runny Chocolate Cake

1 . Melt the chocolate with the butter in a water bath.

2 . Remove from heat and add the sugar, flour and eggs, one by one. Pour into lightly buttered individual ovenproof serving glasses.

3 . Bake at 180°C/350°F/gas mark 4 for about 10 minutes. The centre of the cake should remain runny.

- 500 g/1 lb 2 oz mangoes
- juice of ½ lemon
- 125 g/4 ⅓ oz/⅝ c sugar
- 2 cm/⅘ inch piece ginger root
- 12 cl/4 fl oz/½ c water

MAKES 75 CL/1 ½ PT/3 C
PREPARATION: 10 MIN
COOKING: 5 MIN

Spiced bananas au gratin:

- 4 bananas
- 15 g/½ oz/1 tbsp butter
- 15 g/5 fl oz/⅔ c whipping cream
- 20 cl/6 ¾ fl oz/⅘ c orange juice
- 4 eggs
- 5 cl/1 ⅔ fl oz/ 3 ⅓ tbsp rum
- 100 g/3 ½ oz/ ½ c brown sugar
- ½ tsp ground cinnamon

SERVES: 4 TO 8
PREPARATION: 10 MIN
COOKING: 20 MIN

Mango and Ginger Sorbet

1 . Prepare a syrup. Mix the water and sugar in a large saucepan. Bring to a boil. Reduce the heat and simmer for 5 minutes. Cool to room temperature, then refrigerate 1 hour.

2 . Peel and grate the ginger root. Peel the mangoes and remove the pit. Cut the fruit into large pieces and process until smooth.

3 . Add the lemon juice, grated ginger and cooled syrup.

4 . Pour the preparation into an ice cream maker and freeze according to the manufacturer's instructions. Transfer the ice cream into a recipient of your choice and freeze for at least 3 hours.

5 . Serve with spiced bananas au gratin.

Spiced Bananas au Gratin

1 . Peel the bananas, cut in half lengthwise. Put them in a buttered gratin dish.

2 . In a large bowl, beat the eggs, then add the sugar, rum, orange juice and cream.

3 . Pour over the bananas. Bake at 180°C/350°F/gas mark 4 for about 20 minutes. Serve warm.

Rose-flavoured Cantaloupe Sorbet

- 800 g/1 ¾ lb cantaloupe
- 150 g/5 ¼ oz/¾ c sugar
- juice of 1 lemon
- 3 tbsp crème de rose or rose liqueur

MAKES 75 CL/1 ½ PT/3 C
PREPARATION: 10 MIN

1 . Peel the cantaloupe and remove the seeds. Cut the fruit into pieces. Process until smooth.

2 . Add the sugar, lemon juice and crème de rose and blend for a few more minutes.

3 . Pour the preparation into an ice cream maker and freeze according to the manufacturer's instructions.

4 . Transfer the ice cream into a recipient of your choice and freeze for at least 3 hours.

5 . Serve this sorbet with small balls of various kinds of melon (cantaloupe, honeydew, watermelon, etc.).

Twists

Crème de rose contains about 18% alcohol. Replace with rose syrup if you are making this for your children.

Ingredients

- 3 pears
- 250 g/9 oz/1 ¼ c sugar
- 30 cl/10 fl oz/1 ¼ c water
- 2 cardamom pods
- 2 cloves

MAKES 50 CL/1 PT/2 C
PREPARATION: 15 MIN
COOKING: 1 HOUR TO
1 HOUR 10 MIN

Caramel cups:

- 400 g/14 oz/2 c sugar
- 12 cl/4 fl oz/½ c water

MAKES 6 CUPS
PREPARATION: 30 MIN
COOKING: 20 MIN

Spiced Pear Sorbet

1 . Peel the pears. Put in a pot and cover with water. Add the sugar and heat to poach the pears.

2 . Cook uncovered for 30 to 40 minutes. Keep the poaching liquid. Reduce it over medium heat for 30 minutes and then strain. Remove the pears and core them.

3 . Process the pears and the syrup until smooth. Cool to room temperature, then refrigerate 1 hour.

4 . Place all these ingredients with the other ingredients in the blender.

5 . Process for about 30 seconds, until you get a frothy mixture.

6 . Pour the preparation into an ice cream maker and freeze according to the manufacturer's instructions. Transfer the ice cream into a recipient of your choice and freeze for at least 3 hours.

7 . Serve in caramel cups.

Caramel Cups

1 . Heat the water and sugar in a saucepan until you get a caramel. When it is the right colour, remove from heat and cool for 1 minute.

2 . Choose bowls that are the size and shape you want and turn them over. Cut pieces of aluminium foil to wrap them up. Oil the paper using a pastry brush.

3 . Pour the caramel on these overturned foil-covered bowls. Cool before removing from the moulds.

Ingredients

- 200 g/7 oz raspberries
- 100 g/3 ½ oz meringue crumbs
- 2 tbsp sugar
- 40 cl/13 ½ fl oz/ 1 ⅔ c whipping cream

SERVES: **8** TO **10**
PREPARATION: **20** MIN

Quick Raspberry Vacherin

1 . Whip the cream. Place the whipping cream, the bowl and the beaters in the refrigerator for a half an hour or in the freezer for 10 to 15 minutes, so they are very cold.

2 . Pour the cream into the bowl of a mixer and beat at high speed until it forms peaks. Add the sugar a little before stopping the beater.

3 . Wash and pat dry the raspberries. Add the raspberries and meringue crumbs to the whipped cream and mix delicately.

4 . Pour into a mould, cover with aluminium and freeze for at least 3 hours.

Frozen Chocolate Chestnut Cake

- 3 egg whites
- 25 cl/8 ½ fl oz/
  1 c whipping cream
- 50 g/1 ¾ oz/⅖ c icing
  sugar
- 300 g/10 ½ oz chestnut
  cream
- 100 g/3 ½ oz candied
  chestnut pieces
- a few whole candied
  chestnuts

Chocolate sponge cake:

- 4 eggs
- 125 g/4 ⅓ oz/⅝ c sugar
- 110 g/3 ⅓ oz/⅞ c flour
- 1 tbsp sifted cocoa
  powder

SERVES: 8 TO 10
PREPARATION: 30 MIN
COOKING: 15 TO 20 MIN

1 . Beat the egg whites until stiff but not dry.

2 . Whip the cream until it forms soft peaks (see page 68).
Add the icing sugar a little before stopping the beater.

3 . Mix the whipped cream into the chestnut cream. Fold in the
egg whites and the candied chestnut pieces. Refrigerate.

4 . Prepare the chocolate sponge cake: Separate the eggs.

5 . Beat the yolks until thick and pale. Add the flour and cacao.
Beat the egg whites until stiff but not dry. Fold in to the batter.

6 . Line a baking sheet with greaseproof paper and spread the batter on
the baking sheet. Bake at 180°C/400°F/gas mark 6 for 15 to 20 minutes.
Cool to room temperature.

7 . Line a bread pan with greaseproof paper. Cut strips of sponge cake
the size of your mould. Alternate layers of sponge cake with layers of the
chestnut mixture.

8 . Decorate with a few whole candied chestnuts. Freeze for at least
3 hours.

Frozen Nougat with Berry Sauce

- 120 g/4 ¼ oz/⅝ c sugar
- 100 g/3 ½ oz/ generous ½ c honey
- 3 eggs
- 80 g/2 ⅘ oz/⅔ c unsalted pistachios
- 150 g/5 ¼ oz/1 c whole almonds
- 50 cl/1 pt/2 c whipping cream

Berry sauce:

- 400 g/14 oz mixed berries
- 100 g/3 ½ oz/½ c sugar

SERVES: 8 TO 10
PREPARATION: 40 MIN
COOKING: 5 MIN

1 . Toast the pistachios and the almonds in a skillet with 50 g/1 ¾ oz/¼ cup sugar. Process in a food processor.

2 . Separate the eggs. Heat the honey in a small saucepan. Beat the egg whites until stiff but not dry. Add the heated honey.

3 . Beat the egg yolks with the remaining sugar in a large bowl until thick and pale.

4 . Pour the cream into the bowl of a mixer and beat at high speed until it forms peaks. Mix together the beaten egg whites, the yolks, the sugar, the whipped cream and the caramelized nuts.

5 . Pour the preparation into a loaf pan covered with aluminium foil. Freeze for at least 3 hours.

6 . Just before serving, prepare the berry sauce by processing the fruit together with the sugar to get a smooth sauce. Serve the frozen nougat doused with the berry sauce.

Twists

Feel free to add candied fruit to the nougat, such as candied cherries or orange peel. You can also change the fruit sauce to go with the season. Mangoes, apricots and peaches all go very well with frozen nougat.

Honey, Ginger and Lemongrass Parfait

- 5 eggs
- 120 g/4 ¼ oz/⅝ c sugar
- 60 g/2 oz/⅕ c honey
- a few pieces of candied ginger (optional)
- 120 g/4 ¼ oz mascarpone
- 1 tsp ground ginger
- 1 tsp lemongrass powder

SERVES: 8
PREPARATION: 15 MIN
COOKING: 5 MIN

1 . Beat the egg yolks with the sugar until thick and pale.

2 . Melt the honey in a small saucepan. Add it to the egg yolk mixture with the mascarpone and the spices.

3 . Beat the egg whites until stiff but not dry. Fold into the previous mixture.

4 . Pour into individual ramekins, top with a few pieces of candied ginger (optional) and freeze for 2 to 3 hours.

Did you know?

Lemongrass adds a slight citrus flavour to dishes. It is a traditional ingredient in Asian cuisine. You can use it to marinate fish or meat, or to flavour green mint tea, like the kind made in Morocco.

Pink Grapefruit and Ginger Granita

- 50 cl/1 pt/2 c fresh grapefruit juice
- 100 g/3 ½ oz/½ c sugar
- 2 cm/⅘ inch piece ginger root
- 1 tsp ground ginger

SERVES: 6
PREPARATION: 10 MIN

1 . Pour the sugar in the fresh grapefruit juice and mix well to dissolve it.

2 . Peel the ginger root and grate finely.

3 . Add the ground ginger and fresh ginger to the grapefruit juice.

4 . Steep for 1 hour, then strain through a fine sieve.

5 . Put the mixture in the freezer and freeze for about 1 ½ hours.

6 . Scrape and stir with a fork, crushing any lumps, and return to the freezer. Repeat the operation ½ hour later.

7 . Serve in large glasses.

Did you know?

Ginger is a tropical plant related to orchids that comes from India. For Indians, this is a fundamental plant and a universal remedy. Ginger helps ease nausea and vomiting caused by motion sickness, seasickness and pregnancy. It relieves minor digestive troubles. It helps fight the symptoms of colds and flu, migraine headaches and rheumatism pain.

Ingredients

- 6 tbsp green tea
- 150 g/5 ¼ oz/¾ c sugar
- 1 bunch fresh mint

SERVES: **6** TO **8**
PREPARATION: **15** MIN
COOKING: **10** MIN

Mint Tea Granita

1 . Bring 50 cl/1 pint/2 cups water to a boil. Put the green tea and the mint in a tea pot and add the boiled water. Steep for 10 minutes.

2 . Strain. Add the sugar and mix well to dissolve.

3 . Cool to room temperature, then refrigerate. Put the tea mixture in the freezer and freeze for about 1 ½ hours.

4 . Scrape and stir with a fork, crushing any lumps, and return to the freezer. Repeat the operation ½ hour later.

5 . Serve in large glasses.

Tips and Tricks

Did you know that if you throw a few fresh mint leaves in a vase, your bouquet will last longer? If you live in a flat, grow mint on your balcony. This robust plant proliferates! You don't have to start from seed. Instead, get yourself a few stems and put them in a glass of water until they form roots. Then you can plant them.

Orange-flavoured Coffee Granita

- 30 cl/10 fl oz/ 1 ¼ c espresso
- 50 g/1 ¾ oz/¼ c sugar
- zest of 1 orange

SERVES: 6
PREPARATION: 15 MIN
COOKING: 5 MIN

1 . Prepare a syrup. Mix 10 cl/3 ⅓ fl oz/⅔ cup of water with the sugar in a large saucepan. Bring to a boil, reduce the heat and simmer for 5 minutes. Cool to room temperature.

2 . Make fresh coffee, add the orange zest while the coffee is still hot, and steep until it cools.

3 . Strain through a fine sieve. Mix the coffee and the syrup.

4 . Put the mixture in the freezer and freeze for about 1 ½ hours.

5 . Scrape and stir with a fork, crushing any lumps, and return to the freezer. Repeat the operation ½ hour later.

6 . Serve in large glasses.

Did you know?

Coffee is said to have originated in Ethiopia. There is a fine legend about its discovery. During a forest fire, the coffee trees gave off a delicious aroma. Witnesses of the fire recuperated the roasted beans, crushed them and made a drink from them. And thus coffee was born.

Clementine and Star Anise Granita

- 50 cl/1 pt/2 c clementine juice
- 100 g/3 ½ oz/½ c sugar
- 3 pieces star anise

SERVES: **6** TO **8**
PREPARATION: **10** MIN
COOKING: **5** MIN

1 . Prepare a syrup. Mix 10 cl/3 ⅓ fl oz/⅖ cup water with the sugar in a large saucepan. Add the star anise and bring to a boil. Reduce the heat and simmer for 5 minutes. Cool to room temperature, then refrigerate 1 hour.

2 . Add the clementine juice.

3 . Freeze for about 1 ½ hours.

4 . Scrape and stir with a fork, crushing any lumps, and return to the freezer. Repeat the operation ½ hour later.

5 . Serve in large glasses.

Did you know?

Star anise is a medicinal plant used to fight gastrointestinal ailments, and also ease coughing, colds and bad breath!

Ingredients

- 1 large bunch basil
- juice of 1 lemon
- 150 g/5 ¼ oz/¾ c sugar
- 1 egg white
- 50 cl/1 pt/2 c water

MAKES 30 ICE CUBES
PREPARATION: 10 MIN
COOKING: 5 MIN

Strawberry soup:

- 500 g/1 lb 2 oz straw-
  berries
- 50 g/1 ¾ oz/
  ⅖ c icing sugar
- 10 cl/3 ⅓ fl oz/
  ⅖ c orange juice

SERVES: 6
PREPARATION: 10 MIN

Basil Ice Cubes

1 . Prepare a syrup. Mix the water and sugar in a large saucepan. Bring to a boil. Reduce the heat and simmer for 5 minutes. Cool to room temperature, then refrigerate 1 hour.

2 . Stem the basil and wash the leaves. Blend the leaves in a food processor with the lemon juice.

3 . Beat the egg white until stiff. Mix together all the ingredients.

4 . Pour into ice cube trays and freeze for at least 3 hours.

Strawberry Soup

1 . Wash the strawberries and then remove the stems.

2 . Blend them in a food processor with the icing sugar and the orange juice.

3 . Serve in bowls with basil ice cubes.

Tips and Tricks

Prepare the strawberries at the last minute so they keep as many vitamins as possible. Never soak them, and remove the stem only after washing them under running water. Do not serve strawberries too cold, as they will have less taste that way.

Ingredients

- 7 cl/2 ⅓ fl oz/ generous ¼ c mint syrup
- 7 cl/2 ⅓ fl oz/generous ¼ c grenadine
- 7 cl/2 ⅓ fl oz/generous ¼ c anise syrup
- 21 cl/generous 7 fl oz/ scant 1 c water

MAKES **6** ICE LOLLIES
PREPARATION: **10** MIN

Syrup Ice Lollies

1 . Mix each syrup with ⅓ of the water.

2 . Pour the mint water in the bottom of the ice lollies moulds. Freeze for 3 hours.

3 . Remove from the freezer and add the anise water next. Freeze for 3 hours.

4 . Remove from the freezer a final time and add the grenadine water.

5 . Stick sticks in the centre of each one and freeze for 3 more hours.

Ingredients

- 20 cl/6 ¾ fl oz/⅘ c freshly made strawberry juice
- 20 cl/6 ¾ fl oz/⅘ c freshly made raspberry juice
- 20 cl/6 ¾ fl oz/⅘ c freshly made grape juice
- sugar (optional)

MAKES 25 ICE CUBES
PREPARATION: 15 MIN

Fresh Fruit Ice Cubes

1 . Use a centrifuge juicer to make the juices with fresh fruit.

2 . Sweeten them to taste (raspberry may require sugar, and the grape none).

3 . Pour into ice cube trays and freeze for at least 3 hours.

Tips and Tricks

Use these ice cubes to flavour sparkling water or fruit juices. If your children like ice lollies, add a stick in them before freezing.

Ingredients

- 15 cl/5 fl oz/⅔ c freshly squeezed orange juice
- 15 cl/5 fl oz/⅔ c freshly squeezed lemon juice
- 15 cl/5 fl oz/⅔ c freshly squeezed grapefruit juice
- 45 g/1 ½ oz/scant ½ c sugar

MAKES **6** ICE LOLLIES
PREPARATION: **10** MIN

Citrus Ice Lollies

1 . Add 15 g/½ oz/1 tablespoon of sugar to each of the fruit juices. Mix each preparation well in order to dissolve the sugar.

2 . Pour the orange juice into the ice lolly moulds filling them up one third of the way. Freeze for 3 hours.

3 . Remove the ice lollies from the freezer and add the sweetened lemon juice. Freeze for 3 hours.

4 . Remove the ice lollies a final time and pour in the sweetened grapefruit juice.

5 . Stick sticks in the centre of each one and freeze for 3 more hours.

Twists

Using this basic layer principle, you can have fun playing with various flavours: try an assortment of berries, or summer fruit (apricot, peach, grape) for example.

Lemon and Curcuma Ice Cubes

- 15 cl/5 fl oz/⅔ c freshly squeezed lemon juice
- 10 cl/3 ⅓ fl oz/⅖ c water
- 15 g/½ oz/1 tbsp sugar
- 1 pinch of ground curcuma

MAKES 10 ICE CUBES
PREPARATION: 10 MIN

1 . Mix the water, lemon juice, curcuma and sugar. Mix well to dissolve the sugar.

2 . Pour into ice cube trays and freeze for at least 3 hours.

3 . These ice cubes add a nice flavour to sparkling water, rum or freshly squeezed orange juice.

Did you know?

Curcuma comes from Southern Asia. It is used a lot in India, where it is an ingredient in curries. It has a number of uses and virtues, and traditional medicine uses it to treat digestive problems, gastric ulcers, skin ailments. It is also used as an orange-yellow dye, to colour monks robes, for examples.

Index

A

Almonds
    Almond tuiles   54
    Spice cake and almond ice cream 36
Apples
    Granny Smith sorbet   56
    Spiced apples   30
Aubergine bread   6
Avocado sherbet, shrimp and
smoked salmon   10

B

Baklava   38
Bananas
    Spiced bananas au gratin   62
Basil
    Basil ice cubes   84
    Tomato and basil sorbet   6
Bell peppers
    Cold bell pepper soup   12
Berry sauce   72
Biscuits
    Almond tuiles   54
    Biscuit and pralin ice cream   34
    Caramel heart biscuits   46
    Maple syrup cups   58
    Mixed nut biscuits   28
Blackcurrants
    Frozen honey and blackcurrant
    yogurt   42

C

Cake
    Chocolate sponge cake   70
    Frozen chocolate chestnut cake   70
    Runny chocolate cake   60
Cantaloupe
    Rose-flavoured cantaloupe sorbet 64
Caramel   30
    Caramel cups   66
    Caramel heart biscuits   46
    Salt-butter caramel ice cream   30
Charlotte
    Frozen strawberry charlottes   48

Chestnuts
    Frozen chocolate chestnut cake   70
Chocolate
    Chocolate-coconut balls   26
    Chocolate cups   22
    Chocolate sponge cake   70
    Double chocolate bars   18
    Frozen chocolate chestnut cake   70
    Milk chocolate ice cream   16
    Pear and chocolate crumble   14
    Runny chocolate cake   60
    White chocolate ice cream   24
Citrus ice lollies   90
Clementine
    Clementine and star anise granita 82
    Clementine and tarragon sorbet   8
Coconut
    Chocolate-coconut balls   26
    Coconut ice cream   26
Coffee
    Coffee ice cream   20
    Orange-flavoured coffee granita   80
Cones   34
Cornets   34
Crumble
    Pear and chocolate crumble   14
Curcuma
    Lemon and curcuma frozen
    yogurt   44
    Lemon and curcuma ice cubes   92
Custard sauce   14 and following
    How to save   5

E

Edible recipients
    Caramel cups   66
    Chocolate cups   22
    Cornets (cones)   34
    Maple syrup cups   58
Eggplant
    Aubergine bread   6

F

Fig sorbet   58

Fior di latte
    Ice cream   28
Fresh cheese
    Frozen petits suisses with
    raspberries   46
Frozen desserts
    Frozen chocolate chestnut cake   70
    Frozen nougat with berry sauce   72
    Honey, ginger and lemongrass
    parfait   74
    Quick raspberry vacherin   68
Fruit
    Fresh fruit ice cubes   88

G

Ginger
    Honey, ginger and lemongrass
    parfait   74
    Mango and ginger sorbet   62
    Pink grapefruit and ginger granita 76
Granitas, savoury
    Tapanade granita   12
Granitas, sweet
    Clementine and star anise granita 82
    Mint tea granita   78
    Orange-flavoured coffee granita   80
    Pink grapefruit and ginger granita 76
Granny Smith sorbet   56
Grapefruit
    Pink grapefruit and ginger granita 76

H

Hazelnuts
    Biscuit and pralin ice cream   34
    Caramelized hazelnuts   22
    Hazelnut ice cream   22
Honey
    Frozen honey and blackcurrant
    yogurt   42
    Honey, ginger and lemongrass
    parfait   74

I

Ice cream machines   4
Ice cream sandwiches
    Strawberry and white chocolate   24

Ice cream, sweet
    Biscuit and pralin 34
    Coconut 26
    Coffee 20
    Double chocolate bars 18
    Fior di latte 28
    Hazelnut 22
    Matcha green tea 40
    Milk chocolate 16
    Nougat 32
    Orange flower water 38
    Salt-butter caramel 30
    Spice cake and almond 36
    Vanilla 14
    White chocolate 24
Ice cubes
    Basil 84
    Fresh fruit 88
    Lemon and curcuma 92
Ice lollies
    Citrus 90
    Syrup 86

L

Lemon
    Lemon and curcuma frozen
    yogurt 44
    Lemon and curcuma ice cubes 92
    Lemon sorbet 50
Lemongrass
    Honey, ginger and lemongrass
    parfait 74

M

Mango
    Mango and ginger sorbet 62
    Pineapple and mango carpaccio 40
    Sauce 32
Maple syrup cups 58
Matcha green tea ice cream 40
Mint tea granita 78

N

Nougat
    Frozen nougat with berry sauce 72
    Ice cream with mango sauce 32

O

Olives
    Tapanade granita 12
Orange
    Orange-flavoured coffee granita 80
    Orange sorbet 60
Orange flower water ice cream 38

P

Parfait
    Honey, ginger and lemongrass
    parfait 74

Peach sorbet 54
Pear
    Pear and chocolate crumble 14
    Spiced pear sorbet 66
    Spiced poached pears 36
Petits suisses
    Frozen petits suisses with
    raspberries 46
Pineapple
    Pineapple and mango carpaccio 40
    Pineapple sorbet 52
Pralin
    Biscuit and pralin ice cream 34

Q

Quick raspberry vacherin 68

R

Raspberries
    Frozen petits suisses with
    raspberries 46
    Quick raspberry vacherin 68
Rose-flavoured cantaloupe sorbet 64
Runny chocolate cake 60

S

Salmon
    Avocado sherbet, shrimp and
    smoked salmon 10
    Salmon tartar 8
Sauces
    Berry sauce 72
    Custard sauce 5, 14 and following
    Mango sauce 32
Sherbet, savoury
    Avocado sherbet, shrimp and
    smoked salmon 10
Shrimp
    Avocado sherbet, shrimp and
    smoked salmon 10
Sides, savoury
    Aubergine bread 6
    Cold bell pepper soup 12
    Salmon tartar 8
Sides, sweet
    Almond tuiles 54
    Baklava 38
    Caramel heart biscuits 46
    Mixed nut biscuits 28
    Pear and chocolate crumble 14
    Pineapple and mango carpaccio 40
    Runny chocolate cake 60
    Spiced apples 30
    Spiced bananas au gratin 62
    Spiced poached pears 36
    Strawberry soup 84
Sorbet, savoury
    Clementine and tarragon 8
    Tomato and basil 6

Sorbet, sweet
    Fig 58
    Granny Smith 56
    Lemon 50
    Mango and ginger 62
    Orange 60
    Peach 54
    Pineapple 52
    Rose-flavoured cantaloupe 64
    Spiced pear 66
    Strawberry 48
Soup
    Cold bell pepper soup 12
    Strawberry soup 84
Sponge cake, chocolate 70
Star anise
    Clementine and star anise granita 82
Strawberry
    Frozen strawberry charlottes 48
    Strawberry sorbet 48
    Strawberry soup 84
Spice cake and almond ice cream 36
Spiced bananas au gratin 62
Spiced pear sorbet 66
Sundaes
    Iced coffee 20
    Calvados 56
Syrup ice lollies 86

T

Tapanade granita 12
Tarragon
    Clementine and tarragon sorbet 8
Tartar
    Salmon 8
Tea
    Matcha green tea ice cream 40
    Mint tea granita 78
Tomato and basil sorbet 6
Tuiles
    Almond 54
    Maple syrup cups 58

V

Vacherin
    Quick raspberry vacherin 68
Vanilla ice cream 14

W

Whipped cream 68

Y

Yogurt, frozen
    Frozen honey and blackcurrant
    yogurt 42
    Lemon and curcuma frozen
    yogurt 44

Acknowledgements

The author wants to thanks Anna, Pénélope and Lucie Duval,
Christel Cousin and Anne-Françoise Majault,
Monique and Hervé Le Hingrat.

Note: Tabasco and Mikado are registered trademarks ®.

Editorial director: Muriel Villebrun
Editorial coordination: Béatrice Cordonnier
Graphic design: Valérie Ferrer
Translation: Anne Trager

Photoengraving: Photogravure du Pays d'Oc, Nîmes, France
Printing and binding: Delo Tiskarna, Slovenia, Europe

© Romain Pages Publishing, April 2009

British Library Cataloguing in Publication Data available.
ISBN no. 978-1-906909-07-9

Romain Pages Publishing
Lincoln House – 300 High Holborn
London WC1V 7JH
United Kingdom
email: enquiries@romain-pages.co.uk
website: www.romain-pages.co.uk

Romain Pages Éditions
BP 82030 – 1A Parc Arnède
30252 Sommières Cedex
France
email: contact@romain-pages.com
website: www.romain-pages.com